THE FULNESS OF CHRIST

Stephen Kaung

ISBN: 978-1-942521-47-1

Available from:

Christian Testimony Ministry
4424 Huguenot Road
Richmond, Virginia 23235

www.christiantestimonyministry.com

Printed in USA

CONTENTS

These four messages from the book of Revelation were given by Stephen Kaung at the Christian Family Conference in Richmond, Virginia, July 1988. The conference theme was "Pressing On To Fulness." These messages are transcribed and printed here by permission. All scripture quotations are from the New Translation by J.N. Darby unless otherwise indicated.

FULNESS IN RELATION TO THE CHURCH

Dear Heavenly Father, how we do praise and thank Thee that it is through Thy beloved Son that we can have that entrance into Thy very Presence. Our dear Heavenly Father, we do believe that as we gather together in the name of Thy beloved Son, Thou art in our midst; and we do desire to walk very softly before Thee. We ask Thee, O Lord, that Thou will once again reveal Thy Son to us and in us, that we may see Him, that we may possess Him and be possessed by Him, that Thy will may be done in us as it is in heaven. We do commit this time into Thy hands. We pray that Thou will grant to us the spirit of wisdom and revelation. We pray that Thou will strengthen our inward man that we may be able to apprehend with all the saints and be filled to all the fulness of God. In the name of our Lord Jesus. Amen.

The theme of this conference is Pressing On To Fulness. Probably, the first question we would ask is, "What is this fulness? Why must we must press on to fulness?" This fulness that we are talking about is the fulness of God; it is the fulness of the Godhead. Our God is full; He is fulness.

That ye may be filled even to all the fulness of God. (Ephesians 3:19)

Until we all arrive at the unity of the faith and of the knowledge of the Son of God, at the full-grown man, at the measure of the stature of the fulness of Christ. (Ephesians 4:13)

For in him all the fulness of the Godhead was pleased to dwell. (Colossians 1:19)

For in him (Christ) dwells all the fulness of the Godhead bodily; and ye are complete in Him. (Colossians 2:9-10)

When we are talking about this matter of fulness, we are actually focusing upon the fulness of God, the fulness of the Godhead, the fulness of Christ. In one sense, it is beyond our comprehension to know this fulness because if we are able to know this fulness, then we are able to know God fully. But God is infinite. Therefore, on the one hand, it is beyond our comprehension. When Paul touched upon one aspect of this fullness, the love of God, he said: "This love of God is measureless: what height, what depth, what width!" It is something that he could not describe. It is beyond our comprehension. Yet on the other hand, immediately following, it is said: "That ye may be filled even to all the fulness of God." It is beyond our comprehension, and yet it is within our reach. It is something that we do not fully understand, but, thank God, it is something that we can enter into and be filled with. So this really is a mystery.It is a mystery of God.

We are very thankful that this fulness of God has come to us; and the question is: How does this fulness come to us? This fulness comes to us in God's Son. All the fulness of the Godhead dwells in Him; and this One came into the world. The Word incarnated, became flesh, full of grace and truth; and we have contemplated His glory, even as the glory of the only begotten with the Father. In other words, this fulness of God is in His Son. And when His Son came into the world, even though He put on a human form, the form of a slave, the fashion of a man, within that Man there dwelt the fulness of God bodily. It is there. He brought that fulness into the world. He is full of grace and truth. "God so loved the world that He gave His only begotten Son to us." When God gave His Son, He gave us His fulness. As we believe in His Son, we find that, indeed, God has blessed us with every spiritual blessing in the heavenlies in Christ Jesus.

It is true that we are complete in Him, and by complete it means "filled full with Him." It is a fact; it is the truth.It is something that God has given, and it is something that our Lord Jesus has accomplished for us. But for this fulness to become a daily, living experience to us, we must move from position to condition, from potential to possession. It is given, it is ours; but how are we going to experience and to possess it? It is through the operation of the Holy Spirit. Without the Holy Spirit, this fulness is ours positionally, but we are not able to enter into it experientially. Thank God, the Holy Spirit has come; He is given to us. And His responsibility, His work, is to bring us into that fulness, to take that which has been given in Christ Jesus and make it a reality to each one of us in our daily lives. This is what God has done.

God is so full; Christ is so rich that it is impossible for any one person or few people to possess and contain that fulness. That is the reason God is looking for a body, "The church which is the body of Christ, the fulness of him who fills all and in all" (Ephesians 1:22b-23). We need the church, God needs the church, and our Lord Jesus needs the church because it is only in the church, in the body of Christ, that He is able to fill to the full and manifest His glory. This is what the church is ordained or predestinated to be. But how can the church really become what God designed it to be, the fulness of Christ? "Until we all arrive at the unity of the faith and of the knowledge of the Son of God, at the full grown man, at the measure of the stature of the fulness of the Christ"; until God has a glorious church without spot or wrinkle or any of such things, holy and without blemish. How can it be? This is what the Holy Spirit is doing on this earth today.

It is the will of God that we should enter into His fulness; therefore, I believe it is our duty and responsibility to press on to fulness. If we do not press on, it is a matter of unbelief or disobedience on our part. So may the Lord help us as we share together on this matter of fulness that it will not just be a theory for us to talk about. We look to the Lord that, by the power of the Holy Spirit, He will become a reality, not just to us individually, but also to us together, that God may be glorified.

Revelation is the consummation of all the revelations given not only in the New Testament but also in the Old Testament. Revelation is the last book of the Bible, and it gathers up everything that God has revealed and brings us to the final fulfillment. This book is called The Revelation. It is the revelation of Jesus Christ which God has given to Him to be revealed, to be shown to His church. The book of Revelation is the final and the full revelation of our Lord Jesus. It is a book that tells us not only of His fulness but how His fulness fills all things, and it is the last book that exhorts us to press on into fulness.

And I (that is John) turned back to see the voice which spoke with me; and having turned, I saw seven golden lamps, and in the midst of the seven lamps one like the Son of man, clothed with a garment reaching to the feet, and girt about at the breasts with a golden girdle: his head and hair white like white wool, as snow; and his eyes as a flame of fire; and his feet like fine brass, as burning in a furnace; and his voice as the voice of many waters; and having in his right hand seven stars; and out of his mouth a sharp two-edged sword going forth; and his countenance as the sun shines in its power. And when I saw him I fell at his feet as dead; and he laid his right hand upon me, saying, Fear not; I am the first and the last, and the living one: and I became dead, and behold, I am living to the ages of ages, and have the keys of death and of hades. (Revelation 1:12-18)

The book of Revelation begins with a vision.We call it the Patmos vision because the Apostle John, for the Word of God and for the testimony of Jesus, was exiled to that small island. On the Lord's Day, probably, he was sitting on a rock, facing Asia Minor, looking across the sea and thinking of the churches which he loved and labored for before he was exiled. As he was meditating in the Presence of God, the Bible says he "became in the Spirit." Then he heard a voice from behind saying, "What thou seest, write in a book, and send to the seven churches." He turned around and saw that vision.Now brothers and sisters, sometimes when we are occupied with our present conditions and circumstances, it deprives us of a vision. We need to turn away for a time from that which is immediate, that which is current, in order to see the spiritual reality before God.

THE CHURCH IS THE GOLDEN LAMPSTAND

As he turned back, John saw seven golden lampstands, and we know these golden lampstands represent the seven churches in Asia. The Bible uses the lampstand to represent the church because that is what the church is. The church is not the lamp; it is not the light; it is a lampstand. The church never exists for itself. The church exists to contain and uplift the light, and the light is our Lord Jesus. He is the light of the world; He is the light of life. The church is the vessel, the instrument used by God to uplift Christ that He might shine wide and broad and many may come to His light. That is what the church is.

The seven churches in Asia are like seven golden lampstands, and we know gold represents the nature of God. The church is not something earthly. The church is not something of man. Even though it is composed of man, we have to remember it is not man as such; it is the Christ in man. Therefore, it is a golden lampstand. It is full of God, His life and His nature. It is spiritual, it is heavenly, it is Godly and it is of Christ.

THE PATMOS VISION: THE TEN-FOLD MANIFESTATION OF CHRIST

Now John did not see just seven lampstands; he saw One like the Son of Man in the midst of the seven lampstands. That is the Patmos vision. In other words, John saw seven lampstands as the background, but in the foreground there was a Person. He was like the Son of God. Brothers and sisters, this should always be our perspective. When we talk about the church, we must always see that the church is the background and Christ is the foreground. He saw One like the Son of Man. He saw Him in His ten-fold manifestation, and when John saw this vision, he fell down as one dead.

You remember the story of Saul of Tarsus. He was on his way to Damascus, trying to seize those followers of the Lord Jesus, whom he hated, to bring them to Jerusalem to be sentenced. Suddenly, a light from above shown upon him. He was smitten by that light, and he heard a voice: "Saul, Saul, why does thou persecute me?" (Acts 9:4). He mentioned himself that he saw the righteous One. In other words, here was a man on his way to persecute the followers of Jesus, and he met Jesus. But this Jesus of Nazareth, whom he thought was a man to be despised, and even persecuted, he found was the risen Lord, the Christ, the Lord of all. This vision smote him to the ground and transformed his whole being.

Now we would say, surely, this should happen to Saul but not to John. Who is this John? John is one of the first disciples of our Lord Jesus, and he is the last one of the twelve apostles. He followed the Lord all during those three years. He was one of the disciples who knew the Lord most intimately. He knew the Lord as the Lamb of God. He knew the Lord as his Lord, his Master. He was the one loved by the Lord; and, of course, he loved the Lord. He even laid upon the breast of our Lord Jesus. He had such an intimate relationship with the Lord Jesus while He was on earth. I do not believe that any one of us here knows our Lord Jesus more than this man John did. Yet when he saw One like the Son of Man in the midst of the seven golden lampstands, immediately, he fell down as one dead. It is almost like what Daniel said: "When I saw You my beauty turned into corruption." Even though John knew the Lord so well, and that was his beauty, yet, when he saw the Lord in His glory, his beauty turned into corruption. There was almost no life in him. The Lord had to touch him and raise him up and said:

Fear not; I am the first and the last, and the living one: and I became dead, and behold, I am living to the ages of ages, and have the keys of death and of hades. (Revelation 1:18)

Brothers and sisters, do we know the Lord? Thank God, we do know Him. We know Him as the Lamb of God. I believe many of us know Him as our Lord, our Master. But brothers and sisters, if we really see a vision of the risen Lord, of the Lord in glory, we will be like John and fall down as dead. All our beauty will turn into corruption. How much do we really know Him? It says of Him when He was on earth:

He was like a root out of dry ground: he had no form nor lordliness, and when we see him, there is no beauty that we should desire him. He is despised and left alone of men; a man of sorrows, and acquainted with grief, and like one from whom men hide their faces; despised, and we esteemed him not. (Isaiah 53:2-3)

His visage was so marred more than any man and his form more than the children of men. (Isaiah 52:14)

We know Him as the crucified One, despised, rejected, no form, no lordliness, no beauty. They turned away from Him. But here, you find He is the Lord of glory. What a contrast! But, He is the same One. The crucified One is the One now in glory.

One Like Son Of Man

John said he saw One like the Son of Man. The Son of Man is a title that our Lord Jesus took upon Himself while He was on earth. He always called Himself the Son of Man. It is a name in the days of His humiliation. He is God; and yet He became man, just like us. The Son of Man also means He is the beginning of a new mankind. Man had fallen, come short of the glory of God, of the purpose that God had created him for. But here is a man called the Son of Man, and He is the One who satisfies God's heart as man. He is the Man of God's own heart. He is the perfect Man. He is the beginning of a new mankind, and this Man is in glory. Thank God, we have a Man in glory. In the original, there is not that article "the." It says, "Looks like Son of Man." The Son of Man is His personal name; but when you do not have that article, just Son of Man, it tells us of the characteristics of that manhood. So here, it is more in the sense of the characteristics of that Man. He is the Son of Man; and, as Man, He has fully satisfied God's heart; as Man He is the only One worthy to be taken to the Presence of God. No one can see the face of God. No one can enter into the Presence of God. If you try, you will be smitten to death because you are not worthy. God is holy and you are unholy. But here is a Man, Who is so holy, so perfect, that He has the qualification, the worthiness, to enter into heaven into the very Presence of God and to stay there because He is worthy. He is the only Man in glory.

There is another meaning to this title John gave: "Like Son of Man." It means that He is not only there alone as the Man, the Son of Man, but He is there as our representative. He is there to bring many sons into glory. What characterizes Him as the Son of Man will characterize many men; and He will bring many men into glory. That gives us hope. Thank God, there is a Man in glory; and that guarantees us, assures us, that one day, He will bring us into glory.

Full Of Righteousness

This Man is clothed with a garment reaching to the feet. Garment in the Scripture always signifies conduct, behavior. In Isaiah, it is said that our righteousnesses are as filthy rags. No matter how righteous we are, or we think we are, it is as filthy rags before God. It cannot cover our nakedness. It is to be completely cast out. But here, our Lord Jesus has a garment reaching down to the feet: He is full of righteousness.

In Exodus 28 the high priest had a cloak of the ephod, a garment, made of blue. It was woven as one piece, without seam, with an opening at the top. The Bible says it could not be rent; it was one piece. In John 19, when they crucified our Lord Jesus, they discovered He wore a seamless body-coat, and it was woven as one piece. In other words, the righteousness of our Lord Jesus is without seam. You cannot find any breakdown in Him. He is all righteous, and His righteousness is not of man, of earth; it is of blue, that is, of heaven. His righteousness is heavenly. Brothers and sisters, the righteousness that we profess to have is earthly;

15

and that kind of righteousness is sometimes very repugnant. But the righteousness of our Lord Jesus is heavenly; it is beautiful.

At the hem of the robe of the high priest there were pomegranates made of blue, purple and red, and golden bells: one pomegranate and one golden bell. As he walked, going into the temple, the bells would ring; it was beautiful. It speaks of the righteousness of our Lord Jesus. The pomegranate is a kind of fruit; but if you open it, it is full of seeds with red, juicy meat. In other words, the Lord Jesus is full of righteousness; and the golden bells are testimony. There is such righteousness in Him that it rings out as a testimony unto God. This is our Lord Jesus: He is full of righteousness.

Brothers and sisters, if we catch a glimpse of that vision, will not our beauty turn into corruption? We think that we are righteous, and even though, sometimes, by the grace of God, it may be a fruit of the Spirit and not of ourselves, yet it is not like a pomegranate full. It is just here a little, there a little; and when we see Christ, full of righteousness, we are convicted. We need His resurrection life to raise us up that we may be righteous as He is righteous.

Full Of Love

He is girt about at the breast with a golden girdle. Usually, a girdle is put around the waist because in the old days people wore flowing garments. So when they wanted to work, they had to gird up so it would not interfere with their work. But here, it is very strange because the girdle is not around the waist. It is because the work is already done. The girdle is across His breast, and breast always speaks of compassion, love, and affection. It is a golden girdle. In other words, it is divine love, agape love; it is that selfless love; it is that love that loves to the uttermost; it is first love. Our Lord Jesus is girded with a golden girdle around His breast. He is full of love and compassion.

Righteousness and compassion are incompatible to us because righteousness demands judgment but compassion cries for mercy. Sometimes, we try to be righteous, and we become merciless, we become judgmental.

But then, sometimes, we try to be loving and compassionate, and we become indulgent and even lose the sense of righteousness. But our Lord Jesus is full of righteousness and full of compassion; and these two blend together, work together. This is what the cross tells us. There on the cross, we see righteousness. We do not know what righteousness is until we see the cross. It is there you find the righteousness of God. When His beloved Son became a sin offering for us, God could not spare even His only Beloved because He is righteous. That is the sense of righteousness. But at the same time, we find it is love. The cross is a symbol of love. "For God so loved the world, that He gave His only begotten Son...." Christ so loved us that He gave Himself for us. Here is righteousness and love flowing together. This is our Lord.

Full Of Wisdom

His hair is white like white wool, as snow. According to Proverbs, we know that white hair, hoary hair, grey hair is the crown of glory of the old man because, normally speaking, a person with white hair should be one full of

18

experiences, and experience gives us wisdom. So white hair speaks of wisdom, but, unfortunately, it is not always so.But here, our Lord Jesus' hair is so white like snow. He is full of wisdom; He is wisdom personified. His wisdom is not from beneath; His wisdom is from above.

But the wisdom from above first is pure, then peaceful, gentle, yielding full of mercy and good fruit, unquestioning, unfeigned. (James 3:17)

That is our Lord Jesus. Oh, how wise He is! We need that wisdom.

Full Of Discernment

His eyes are as a flame of fire. He is full of discernment, spiritual discernment. You do not need to tell Him; He sees you through and through. When He saw Simon, He looked through that man. He saw the potential there; He saw what God could make out of him and He said, "You are Peter; you shall be called Peter, a stone." When our Lord Jesus was being judged, Peter was warming himself in the court. There he denied the Lord and our Lord just turned back and looked at him. It was not a hateful look;

it was a look of compassion, a piercing look, and it brought Peter into repentance. Our Lord Jesus is full of discernment. Dear brothers and sisters, if you know the Lord as such, will you not fall down as dead? But thank God, His eyes are as a flame of fire; it burns, it consumes, it purifies and it glorifies.

Full Of Righteous Judgment

His feet are like fine brass, as burning in a furnace. Feet speak either of walk or stand. Brass speaks of judgment, but it is judgment unto redemption. The brazen altar in the temple speaks of judgment; and yet it speaks of redemption too. It is judged that it may be redeemed. What our Lord Jesus sees with His eyes, He puts His feet upon. He tramples it under His feet; He judges it.And His judgment is righteous because in the gospel of John He said He does not judge according to man; He does not judge according to what can be seen; He judges according to God. How we need that judgment that we may be redeemed!

His Voice As Many Waters

His voice is as the voice of many waters.
Brothers and sisters, it was prophesied in Isaiah
42 and then fulfilled in Matthew 12 that when
our Lord Jesus was on earth, no one heard His
voice on the street. He did not strive; He did not
raise His voice. A broken reed He will not break,
a smoking flax He will not quench until He brings
judgment into this world (see Isaiah 42:2-4). In
glory, His voice is as the voice of many waters:
majestic and full of authority. That is the reason
why, in Hebrews 3, it is said: "Today, if ye hear
His voice, harden not your hearts."

His Hand Of Supply

He has in His right hand seven stars. Hands
speak of work and right hand speaks of power,
preeminence, honor. Our Lord Jesus holds the
seven stars in His right hand. The seven stars are
explained to us as the seven angels of the seven
churches. Now even though there are various
interpretations about these seven stars, the
angels, we know the word in the original simply
means "messengers." There are celestial

messengers and terrestrial messengers; and personally, I think these are terrestrial messengers because they received the letters from the Lord. They represented those who are spiritually responsible for the churches; and remember they are in the right hand of our Lord Jesus. In other words, the Lord says: "I am your support, I am your supply. My grace is sufficient for you. You can depend upon Me as you fulfill your responsibility."

Full Of Power

Out of His mouth there is a sharp two-edged sword going forth. In Hebrews 4:12, the Word of God is like a sharp two-edged sword, penetrating, dividing the soul and the spirit to the discerning of the thoughts and intents of the heart. Everything is naked before God. The word there is not logos; the word there is rhema. It is God's Presence speaking to us personally, and when God speaks to us personally, it is like a two-edged sword that will divide the soul and the spirit and will deliver. He is full of power.

Full Of Health And Beauty

His face, His countenance is as the sun shining in its power. In Psalm 42, it says, "the health of my countenance," or "the salvation of my countenance." The countenance, the face, actually reveals your health. If you are healthy, you have a rosy cheek. It reveals your health or your beauty within. Our Lord Jesus is full of health and beauty.

THE CHURCH TO POSSESS THE FULNESS OF CHRIST

This ten-fold description tells us of the risen Lord, of the Son over His house, of our great high priest, of the Man in glory. This is the vision that John saw on that island, but it is given to him in connection with the seven golden lampstands. It is true, God's purpose is for us to see the glory of our Lord Jesus: the moral glory of the Son of Man and the eternal glory of the Son of God. God wants us to see Him, but remember, it is in relation to the church. He wants us to see the church too. You cannot see Him without seeing the seven golden lampstands; and that means what He is is not just for us to con-template, but for us to possess. What He is is revealed for us and is towards us. He wants us to be filled with His fulness. That is what the church ought to be. The church is the body of Christ, the fulness of Him who fills all and in all. He reveals Himself to His church.

Brothers and sisters, what is revelation? What is revelation for? Revelation is never given for us just to contemplate, to speculate. Revelation is given that it may become our vocation. Our God is a practical God. He does not give us revelation just so we can talk about it and boast of it. Revelation is given with a responsibility. It is given that we may be involved in that vision, that we may become part of that vision, that vision may be turned into vocation. Revelation either fulfills or condemns. If we respond to revelation, it brings fulfillment; but if we do not respond to revelation, it condemns us. It is a very serious matter.

In each of the seven letters to the seven churches, the Lord reminded them of Himself. What is the Lord looking for in the church? He is not looking for work; He is not looking for labor; He is not looking for knowledge; He is not looking for many things; He is looking for Himself. He tells every church: This is what I am; this is what I have revealed to you; and where am I in your midst?You have this, you have that, you have many, many things, which are good; but what do you have of Me?

To the church in Ephesus He said: "You have all these things, but I am against you because you have left your first love." First love, He is first love; but where is He?

To the church in Smyrna, a suffering church, He said: "Be faithful even unto death because I am the first and the last, and I am the One who became dead and I am living for evermore. This is what I am. Be faithful to the very end."

To the church in Pergamos He said: "I am the One that has the two-edged sword." In other words, that church had become so complicated; He wanted them to return to the simplicity and the sincerity of Christ Jesus.

To the church in Thyatira, He was the One whose eyes are of flaming fire and His feet like fine brass. The Lord looked at that church and saw that it was all of the flesh, and He wanted to divide the soul and the spirit. He said: "Those who do not know these depths of Satan, hold on to what you have."

To the church in Sardis, He said: "I am the One who has the seven stars and of the seven spirits, but where is life in your midst?"

To the church in Philadelphia He said: "I am the holy One, the truth, He who has the key of David. Hold on; hold fast that no one will take away your crown."

To the church in Laodicea He said: "I am the Amen, the faithful and true witness, the beginning of the creation." But He said: "There is no reality in your midst; I am outside of the door."

Brothers and sisters, the fulness of Christ is revealed to the church. This is our inheritance. But it is revealed that we may possess it to the glory of God. Therefore, we must press on to fulness. May the Lord help us.

Shall we pray:

Dear Heavenly Father, oh, how we praise and thank Thee that it does please Thee to reveal Thy Son in us, not just a little bit, but the fulness of Christ to the church. Oh, what a privilege; but Father, we do acknowledge that it is a great responsibility. We have to acknowledge that we have failed. We have failed to respond to Thy beloved Son.There is much in us, but it is not Thee.Lord, we have very little of Thy Son. We just pray, Lord, that Thou would create within us a repentant, a contrite spirit; that Thou will create within us a hunger and thirst after righteousness. Oh, we do pray that Thou will so empty us that Thou may fill us with Christ Jesus; oh, that He may be all and in all, that Thy will may be done and Thy glory may be manifested. We ask in the name of our Lord Jesus. Amen.

FULNESS IN RELATION
TO THE WORLD

Revelation 5:1-14 And I saw on the right hand of him that sat upon the throne a book, written within and on the back, sealed with seven seals. And I saw a strong angel proclaiming with a loud voice, Who is worthy to open the book, and to break its seals? And no one was able in the heaven, or upon the earth, or underneath the earth, to open the book, or to regard it. And I wept much because no one had been found worthy to open the book nor to regard it.And one of the elders says to me, Do not weep. Behold, the lion which is of the tribe of Juda, the root of David, has overcome so as to open the book, and its seven seals.

And I saw in the midst of the throne and of the four living creatures, and in the midst of the elders, a Lamb standing, as slain, having seven horns and seven eyes, which are the seven Spirits of God which are sent into all the earth: and it came and took it out of the right hand of him that sat upon the throne. And when it took the book, the four living creatures and the twenty-four elders fell before the Lamb, having each a harp and golden bowls full of incenses, which are the prayers of the saints. And they sing a new song, saying, Thou art worthy to take the book, and to open its seals; because thou hast been slain, and hast redeemed to God, by thy blood, out of every tribe, and tongue, and people, and nation, and made them to our God kings and priests; and they shall reign over the earth.

And I saw, and I heard the voice of many angels around the throne and the living creatures and the elders; and their number was ten thousands of ten thousands and thousands of thousands; saying with a loud voice, Worthy is the Lamb that has been slain, to receive power, and riches, and wisdom, and strength, and honour, and glory, and blessing. And every creature which is in the heaven and upon the earth and under the earth, and those that are upon the sea, and all things in them, heard I saying, To him that sits upon the throne, and to the Lamb, blessing, and honour, and glory, and might, to the ages of ages.

And the four living creatures said, Amen; and the elders fell down and did homage.

Shall we pray:

Thou art worthy, O Lamb of God. Thou alone art worthy because Thou has taken that book to open it. Oh, how we worship Thee because Thou art the Victor of Calvary. It is because of Thee that we are redeemed. It is because of Thee that all things are reconciled to the fulness of God. So Lord, as we gather together, we do come before Thee with a worshipping spirit. We worship Thee. May Thy name be highly exalted in the midst of the congregation. We ask in the name of our Lord Jesus. Amen.

The book of Revelation is the revelation of Jesus Christ. It reveals to us the fulness of Christ in various relationships. We have shared on the fulness of Christ in relation to the church, and now we would like to see the fulness of Christ in relation to the world. The scene has changed. In the first chapter, John was on the island of Patmos, and on the Lord's Day he was in the spirit. He heard a voice behind him, and when he turned around he saw that vision. In chapter 4 of the book of Revelation, he heard a voice say, "Come up hither." He became in the spirit; he saw an open heaven, and in that heaven he saw a scene. We believe that chapter 4 is the scene of the glory of the Creator. Our God is the Creator; He created all things. This chapter is very quickly followed by chapter 5, and we believe it is the glory of the Redeemer.

GOD'S WILL IN CREATION

The first question we would like to ask is: "What is the creation for?" Scientists ask the question, "What is creation?" But we ask the question, "What is creation for?" They want to know what, but we want to know why. Why are these things created? Why are the things in heaven, on earth, in the sea, and underneath the earth created? Why are we created? Why are the angels created? Why are all things created? We believe that all things do not exist for themselves. They exist for a reason; and we would like to know the reason why. In chapter 4, the twenty-four elders, the elders of the universe, knew why; and they told us. In their worshipping God, the Creator, they said:

Thou art worthy, O our Lord and our God, to receive glory and honour and power; for thou has created all things, and for thy will they were, and they have been created. (Revelation 4:11)

God created all things; and He created all things for His will, or in some versions it says, "for His pleasure." There is the pleasure of God; there is the will of God; and it is according to the good pleasure of His will that He created all things. Nothing is created out of the will of God.There is a will that controls the creation that tells us why all things are created.

Who, (that is the Son of God's love) is image of the invisible God, firstborn of all creation; because in him were created all things, the things in the heavens and the things upon the earth, the visible and the invisible, whether thrones, or lordships, or principalities, or authorities: all things have been created by him and for him. And he is before all, and all things subsist together by him. And he is the head of the body, the assembly; who is the beginning, firstborn from among the dead, that he might have the first place in all things. (Colossians 1:15-18)

What is the will of God in creation? The will of God in creation is that His beloved Son may have the first place in all things. God created all things for His Son. God created all things to give all things as His gift to His Son, that His Son might have the first place in all things, that all things might glorify His beloved Son. This is the why of creation. All things are created for the Son. You and I are created for the Son. That is the reason for creation.

God created all things in His Son. When the translators translated the Bible, they found it very difficult to say that all things were created in Him, because how can all things be created in Him? So they used the word by Him; but, actually, we find the by Him later on. All things were created in Him, by Him and for Him.In other words, He was the designer, the architect; He designed all things. He was the builder, the contractor; He built all things. And He was the owner, the master, the Lord of all things. When all things were created, they were created by our Lord Jesus designing them; and in designing all things, all things do manifest His wisdom and, to a certain degree, His character. He was the One who actually created all things. By Him all things were created, and that demonstrated His power and His authority. He created all things by His Word. He spoke the Word, and it was done. What power! What authority! And after all things were created, they were His property, His inheritance. He was the owner of all things.

Dear brothers and sisters, I do believe, when all things were first created, there was harmony. In the beginning when all things were created, they really reflected the glory of the Son. When God laid the foundation of the earth, the morning stars sang and the sons of God shouted for joy (see Job 38:7). In other words, there was harmony there. When God created all things, all things were in oneness: they gave the glory to God, and they manifested the glory of the Son. It was just a beautiful, harmonious scene. All things were created according to God's will, and God's will was done in the beginning.

THE WILL OF GOD CHALLENGED

But at a certain point in time, something happened. That will of God was challenged. Pride entered into the heart of the archangel Lucifer, the brilliant star. He became ambitious. He wanted to put all things under himself. He wanted to rule over all things. In other words, he wanted to take the place of the Son. We can see this hinted in Isaiah 14 and Ezekiel 28. God had put this archangel into a very high position. He was created with beauty and gifts, and God gave him dominion to rule. Yet he was not satisfied to reflect and give glory to the Son of God. He wanted to take the place of God's Son. But our God is a jealous God. He will not allow anyone to challenge His will; He will not allow anyone to challenge His beloved Son. That is the reason why this archangel was cast out of heaven, and he turned himself into Satan, the adversary of God. When he rebelled against God, he took one-third of the angelic hosts with him into rebellion, and the dominion that was under him entered into corruption and ruin. Evidently, this universe of ours was at one time given to him to rule for God's Son. That is the reason why our universe had entered into ruin and corruption and had become aimless, purposeless and disintegrated.That was the scene in the beginning of the book of Genesis.

MAN'S MISSION

Thank God, He did not give up His will. We find that God began to work. The whole earth was covered with water, and the Spirit of God hovered over the deep. With His word He repaired this ruined earth in six days to make it habitable; and on the sixth day He created man. He created man in His own image, and there is a reason for that. He gave man dominion over the fowls of the sky, over the beasts of the field and over the fishes of the sea. He gave man the commission of subduing all things. Brothers and sister, here we find a hint. God created man with a specific reason, and that reason is related to His will: God wants to use man as His vessel and instrument to subdue all things, to bring all things back to the feet of the Son of God. All things have drifted away from the center and disintegrated. Our Lord Jesus is the cohesive force that brings all things into one. He was the center; but because of the rebellion that happened in the universe, all things disintegrated and drifted apart. They lost their meaning and fell into ruin and corruption and rebellion. They did not manifest the glory of the Son of God anymore. Then God created man. God had a commission for man that he would bring all things back to the Son of God that the Son of God might have the first place in all things. So man's mission was to subdue all things, to take all things out of the hands of the enemy and bring them back to Christ. What a creation! What a commission!

MAN'S FALL

Unfortunately, in Genesis 3, we find man was tempted by the tempter. Man was tempted to be self-centered; man was tempted to pride; man was tempted to ambition for himself, just like what had happened to that archangel in the beginning. Man fell into temptation, and instead of being used by God to bring all things back to the Son, man joined the enemy's camp and the earth was cursed. Man was cast out of the garden of Eden. It was as if God's will was frustrated.

God's Work of Reconciliation

Did God give up? Thank God, our Lord Jesus said, "My Father worketh until now and I work." God started to do the work of recovery; and in the fulness of time, He sent His beloved Son into this world to become a man.

But now we see not yet all things subjected to him, but we see Jesus, who was made some little inferior to angels on account of the suffering of death, crowned with glory and honour; so that by the grace of God he should taste death for everything. (Hebrews 2:8b-9)

In the fulness of time, God sent His Son into this world. We see Jesus. He was made a little lower than the angels because, according to the order of creation, angels occupy a higher order than man. They are more intelligent than man; they are spirit. But here you find the Son of God emptied Himself of the glory, of the honor, of the power that belonged to Him; and He took upon Himself the form of a bondslave, even the fashion of a man. We see Jesus made a little lower than the angels on account of the suffering of death. Jesus came into this world not to live but to die. He came to die; He came to redeem the world; He came to reconcile all things to His fulness.

Andby him to reconcile all things to itself. (Colossians 1:20)

Some versions put "to Himself." I will not quarrel with that, but I feel "to itself" has a very special meaning, "To reconcile all things to itself." What is that "itself"? The antecedent of "itself" is in verse 19, and it is the fulness of the Godhead. In other words, by Him, that is by Jesus, God is to reconcile all things to the fulness of Him, having made peace by the blood of His cross. By the blood of the cross, He made peace; and this peace is not just for man. When we think of the blood of the cross, of course, we think of ourselves and how our sins are atoned. Thank God for that. But here he said, "By him, whether the things on the earth or the things in the heavens." The blood of the cross of our Lord Jesus has a much farther, much greater significance. It is not only to reconcile us to God's fulness but it is to reconcile all things, whether in heaven or on earth.

And you, (that is us) who once were alienated and enemies in mind by wicked works, yet now has it reconciled in the body of his flesh through death; to present you holy and unblamable and irreproachable before it. (Colossians 1:21-22)

In some other versions it is "Him"; but it is the same. It is Him, but it is "it." In other words, it is that fulness.

Dear brothers and sisters, there on the cross, our Lord Jesus has laid the foundation of the reconciling of all things back to His fulness. How far-reaching an effect that is. Oh, the precious blood of our Lord Jesus. Oh, the cross of our Lord Jesus. It has not only redeemed us from our sins and transgressions, it has brought us back into the fulness of God that we might become irreproachable, unblamable, holy before the fulness of God. What a salvation this is! Thank God, the foundation is laid. It is the foundation for the reconciling of all things back to the will of God that all things will manifest the glory of God's Son, that all things will be for God's Son, that all things will enter into the fulness of God. That foundation was laid on the cross of our Lord Jesus at Calvary.

The scientists are interested in knowing the physical history of the universe. They want to know the age of the universe; they want to know the extent of the universe; they want to know the formation of the universe; they want to know the change in the universe. They are interested in the physical history of the universe. But what is our interest? Our interest is in the spiritual history of the universe. We know this universe was created in the beginning for God's will, for God's Son; and we also know that something tragic has happened. But, thank God, we also know that through the cross of Calvary the foundation of recovery or restoration of all things has been laid; and now we are interested to see how this is developed.

THE SEALED BOOK

We believe Revelation 5 is the scene of the ascension of our Lord Jesus. It is a replay of the scene of our Lord's ascension. There are many reasons for it. We find the Lamb slain. Our Lord Jesus was the Lamb of God. He came into this world to take away the sin of the world; and there on the cross, that Lamb was slain. But we see that Lamb in heaven, standing before the throne. He is standing. If a lamb is slain, he must lie down.But here this Lamb, slain, and in some versions it says "newly slain", is standing. It speaks of resurrection. But, thank God, even though He is in heaven, He has not changed His personality. The position has changed, but the personality remains the same. He is still the Lamb.

There is a book in the hand of the One who sits upon the throne, and we know the One who sits upon the throne is none other than God, Himself. This book He has in His hand is sealed with seven seals, and we believe it is the title deed of the universe. God owns all things. He has never relinquished His ownership. The title deed is still in His hand. Even though our universe is occupied today by the enemy, he is the usurper. Even though he is called the god of this world, the ruler of this world, yet we know he is a usurper; he is a squatter. He occupies this universe that does not belong to him. All things in this universe still belong to God. It is in His hands.

This book is written within and without. It is God's detailed plan to restore all things to His will; but it is sealed. That plan has not been executed. Nobody knows how God is going to recover His property. God has a plan, but nobody knows it, and nobody is executing it.

THE CHALLENGE TO OPEN THE BOOK

So there was the challenge to the universe. A strong angel with a loud voice that could be heard said, "Who is worthy to open the book and open the seals?" In other words, who is worthy to execute the plan of God? It is a matter of worthiness. It is more than a matter of power; it is a matter of authority. Worthiness is something that is based upon past life and performance. Worthiness means that there is a qualification

proven beyond dispute. Who is worthy to take
that book, open the seals and execute the will of
God to bring all things back to God's will, to
fulness? It was a tremendous challenge! And the
voice was heard not only in heaven but on earth
and underneath the earth. It was a challenge that
went out to every creature, to everything
celestial and terrestrial, visible and invisible, and
there was silence. The whole creation stood still,
waiting for that one; but nobody answered. The
Bible says John wept.

Brothers and sisters, if you know the
meaning of it, I believe you will weep too. This
universe of ours is occupied by the enemy, and
he tries to make it his own, to put his imprint
upon everything. God is actually the owner of it,
but no one is able to execute God's plan to bring
all things back to God's will. Is this a hopeless
situation? Are we hopeless? Is there is no hope
for all creation? All creation groans and groans
under corruption and purposelessness. We
groan in pain and sorrow, having no hope.Is this
something that will continue forever and ever?

Is there no hope?Has God given up His will? Is God defeated?

Brothers and sisters, if you understand the seriousness of the situation, I believe you will weep with John. He wept much, and he was comforted by one of the elders. He said: "Weep not; there is One who is worthy. He is the Lion of the tribe of Judah, the root of David. He has overcome." Immediately, John saw a Lamb standing, as slain. This Lamb stepped forward and took that book from God's hand.

THE LIONIZED LAMB IS WORTHY

The lion is mighty among beasts, which will not turn away from anything (Proverbs 30:30). The lion represents majesty, might and strength. The lamb is just the opposite; it signifies meekness, lowliness and pureness. He is the Lion of the tribe of Judah; but John did not see a lion, he saw a lamb. But brothers and sisters, this Lamb is lionized. While He was on earth, He was a Lamb, helpless, and because of weakness, He was crucified. But now in heaven, He is still the Lamb, but He is lionized. He is full of might, majesty and glory. He is worthy to take the book in His hand because He has overcome on Calvary's cross. He has spoiled principalities and authorities. He has taken them as His captives and made a show of them. He has released us; He has set the captives free. He has opened the gate. Brothers and sisters, our Lord Jesus is worthy. He has proven through His life and in His death that He is worthy. He is the One who is worthy to execute the plan of God. When that thing happened there was worship and praises in the whole universe, as if it is already done. And then you go to chapter 6 where He begins to open the seals.

THE LAMB ANOINTED AS CHRIST

Two things happened when our Lord Jesus ascended to heaven. He took from God that title deed of the universe. This is a fulfillment of the prophecy in Psalm 2: "Ask of Me and I will give the earth for Your inheritance." This is a fulfillment of Psalm 110: "God has made Him a priest after the order of Melchisedek." This is what Peter testified on the day of Pentecost:

What you have seen and heard tells you that God has made Jesus both Lord and Christ.

When our Lord Jesus returned to heaven as the Lamb slain, He was anointed by the Father as Christ, the Christ, the Messiah, the anointed One.When God anointed Him, the oil flowed down as from Aaron's head, and it came down to the skirt. That was Pentecost. Here you find the Lamb has seven eyes and seven horns. Horns represent power; eyes represent wisdom. These seven horns and seven eyes are the seven spirits that are being sent into the world. After the ascension of our Lord Jesus, He received from the Father the power from on high; and there He poured down His Spirit upon this earth. The Holy Spirit is the power of God; the Holy Spirit is the wisdom of God; the Holy Spirit is given to the church. And here the Holy Spirit is sent to the world.

THE KINGDOM OF GOD MANIFESTED ON EARTH

Through the working of the Holy Spirit, many are convicted, brought to repentance and enter into salvation. Thou has redeemed a people out of every tribe, every tongue, every nation; and Thou has made them kings and priests unto God, and they shall reign over the earth. Brothers and sisters, when our Lord Jesus is executing the plan of God in recovering all things, on the one hand, He is calling many people out of every tribe, every nation, every tongue and every people. He has redeemed a people, set them free from the enemy's bondage and from the fear of death, brought them into life, and made them a kingdom, priests unto God. In Revelation 1:5-6, it says He loves us, He has washed our sins by His blood, and He has made us a kingdom, priests unto God. Do you know what this means? This world is occupied by the enemy. He set his kingdom upon this earth. He organized the world into a kingdom of darkness. He put his imprint upon everything in this world. Whether it is political, economic, social, educational or even religious, he has organized the whole world as a cosmos, as a system, as a kingdom of darkness; and he rules over this world. He has absolute power over the whole world.

But then something happened. Our Lord Jesus invaded this world. He came into this world occupied by the enemy. He invaded the occupied territory, He entered into the house, He bound the strong man and He set the prisoners free. And more than that, He laid the foundation; and now, by the power of the Holy Spirit, He is building His kingdom in the occupied territory. Right in the kingdom of darkness, He is building the kingdom of the Son of God's love. Wonderful! Oh, brothers and sisters, this is a kingdom not of the world; this is the kingdom of heaven. This is a spiritual kingdom; this is the true kingdom, the kingdom of the Son of God's love. He has translated us out of the power of darkness and has put us in this kingdom. He has made us kings. We are here to rule for God. We are here to subdue all things to the feet of our Lord Jesus. We are here as priests to worship and to serve God. Think of that! Right in the enemy's territory, God is building His kingdom. Brothers and sisters, what a responsibility! When our Lord Jesus is opening the seals in heaven, His church on earth is carrying out His will.

For this reason take to you the panoply of God, that ye may be able to withstand in the evil day, and, having accomplished all things, to stand. (Ephesians 6:13)

Brothers and sisters, we are in the enemy's territory, and that is the reason why we have to take up the whole armor of God. We have to put on Christ that we may be able to withstand in the evil day. But it is more than withstanding, "and having accomplished all things." Now what does that mean? We are not here just to be on the defensive: the enemy is attacking us and we just try to withstand it. No, it is more than that. "Having accomplished all things, to stand." This means having overcome all things, or it can mean to carry through and to put into execution all that is purposed and called for in spite of opposition. Brothers and sisters, we are the kingdom of God on earth. We are here to carry through, to put into execution, the will and the purpose of God in the face of opposition. That is our mission, our task; and one day, when there is enough spiritual energy generated, the power of darkness will be overturned and the kingdom of

God will be manifested upon this earth. This is what is going on and, thank God, we are in it. We are a part of it.

THE KINGDOM OF DARKNESS REVEALED

That is one side, but there is another thing going on. When our Lord Jesus began to open the seals, you find wars, famine, killings and disaster after disaster. With the opening of the seals, one-fourth of the whole universe is affected. With the sounding of the trumpets, one-third of the universe is destroyed. We find all these disasters coming upon this earth. Now why? What does it mean?

Brothers and sisters, the question is often asked: Is it God who gives us the wars, famine, poverty, sickness, death, sorrows and tears? If God is good, why does He give us all these things? That is always asked. It is true, when our Lord is opening the seals, these things happen on earth; but remember, it is because of the sins of the world. It is because of the resistance, the opposition of the enemy. The enemy has occupied this universe for a long time, and he will not give up. He is making his last stand. All these things are the result of our sins. All these things happening are just revealing the nature of the kingdom of darkness.

When God delivered the children of Israel out of Egypt, Pharoah would not let them go. If he had let the children of Israel go, there would have been no plagues; but he would not let them go. Because of that, plague after plague came upon that land of Egypt until, finally, all the opposition of the enemy was destroyed. Not only were the Egyptians destroyed, but the gods of the Egyptians were destroyed. Those plagues were the gods of the Egyptians; and actually, it just brought out the very nature of the kingdom of Egypt. All the evil nature of that kingdom came out in its fulness when God was trying to deliver His people.

In Matthew 24, our Lord Jesus said there will be wars and rumors of wars, there will be famines, there will be earthquakes, and there will be all these disasters coming. We know as the coming of the Lord draws nearer and nearer, these things will intensify and extend their scope. It is bound to happen; but the Lord said that this is not the end; this is the beginning of birth pains. A woman bearing a child in her womb travails with birth pains when the baby is ready to come out. She will be travailing in pains; and when the time comes closer and closer, the pain intensifies until, finally, the baby is born and she forgets her pain.She rejoices. That is what is happening.

ALL THINGS SUMMED UP ON CHRIST

Brothers and sisters, when our Lord Jesus is restoring all things, the enemy is trying all-out to resist; and that is the reason why all that he is comes out. He is the murderer; he is the deceiver; he is the liar; he is the accuser; he is the wicked one; he is the adversary; he is the dragon; he is the old serpent. All the evil nature of the enemy and of his kingdom begins to be manifested. That is the reason why killing, murdering and all these disasters are happening; that is the opposition of the enemy.

But, thank God, God is using this to bring forth a man child.God is using it to complete us; God is using it to make us full of Christ. When that man child is born, he will be raptured into heaven, and Satan will be thrown upon this earth. There will be the Great Tribulation, the seven bowls of the wrath of God. There will be the last battle of Armageddon, and the false christ and the false prophet will be bound and thrown into the lake of fire. Satan will be bound and put into the bottomless pit for a thousand years, and the kingdom of God will rule upon this earth for a thousand years. After this, Satan will be released temporarily. He will try to tempt the people again. The last rebellion will be put down, the old heaven and old earth will pass away, and the New Jerusalem will descend upon the new earth. This is eternity, and all things will have been summed up in Christ. Isn't that the purpose of God? In Ephesians, it says the purpose of God is to sum up all things in Christ. All things are regathered together in Christ, and all things will speak of the glory of the Son of God. Oh, hallelujah!

Shall we pray:

Dear Heavenly Father, how we worship Thee because Thou art the Creator of the universe. Oh, how we praise Thee because Thou has never given up Thy rights. How we thank and praise Thee that Thy Son is worthy, is worthy to take the book, to open the seals and to bring all things back to Thy fulness. Oh, our Heavenly Father, we do praise and thank Thee that Thou has called us into Thy fulness through Thy Son, by Thy Holy Spirit. We praise and thank Thee we are not only the recipients of Thy grace but Thy grace has such an effect upon us that we may also be used by Thee with Christ in bringing all things to His feet. Oh, we worship Thee, we thank Thee, in the name of our Lord Jesus. Amen.

FULNESS IN RELATION TO THE OVERCOMER

Revelation 12:1-12 And a great sign was seen in the heaven: a woman clothed with the sun, and the moon under her feet, and upon her head a crown of twelve stars; and being with child she cried, being in travail, and in pain to bring forth.

And another sign was seen in the heaven: and behold, a great red dragon, having seven heads and ten horns, and on his heads seven diadems; and his tail draws the third part of the stars of the heaven; and he cast them to the earth. And the dragon stood before the woman who was about to bring forth, in order that when she brought forth he might devour her child. And she brought forth a male son, who shall shepherd all the nations with an iron rod; and her child was caught up to God and to his throne. And the woman fled into the wilderness, where she has there a place prepared of God, that they should nourish her there a thousand two hundred and sixty days.

And there was war in the heaven: Michael and his angels went to war with the dragon. And the dragon fought, and his angels; and he prevailed not, nor was their place found any more in the heaven. And the great dragon was cast out, the ancient serpent, he who is called Devil and Satan, he who deceives the whole habitable world, he was cast out into the earth, and his angels were cast out with him.

And I heard a great voice in the heaven saying, Now is come the salvation and the power and the kingdom of our God, and the authority of his Christ; for the accuser of our brethren has been cast out, who accused them before our God day and night: and they have overcome him by reason of the blood of the Lamb, and by reason of the word of their testimony, and have not loved their life even unto death. Therefore be full of delight, ye heavens, and ye that dwell in them. Woe to the earth and to the sea, because the devil has come down to you, having great rage, knowing he has a short time.

Shall we pray:

Lord, as we continue in Thy presence, we just bow in worship and adoration. How we do praise and thank Thee that Thou has sent Thy beloved Son into the world to be the Lamb of God slain for us. We do praise and thank Thee that Thou has exalted Him far above all, and Thou has given Him a name that is above every name; and to that name every knee shall bow, every tongue confess that Jesus is Lord. Oh, how we praise and thank Thee that Thou has been so gracious to us that we can come to Thee with a willing heart, bowing our knees and acknowledging Thee as our Lord. Oh, Thou art worthy. We worship Thee; and we just pray that as we read Thy Word, that Thy Holy Spirit will breathe again upon it, to make it living and operative in our lives. We do pray that Thou will open our eyes to see, and Thou will touch our heart that we may be fully in tune with Thyself. We want Thy will to be done on earth as it is in heaven. We ask in the name of our Lord Jesus. Amen.

The will of God for us is to press on to fulness. Our God is the God of fulness and His fulness is located in His beloved Son; we are made full in Him. We thank God for the accomplished work of our Lord Jesus. We thank God for the operation of the Holy Spirit that we might enter into that fulness to the glory of God.

We have been looking at the fulness of Christ in the book of Revelation. Now we would like to see the fulness of Christ in relation to the overcomers. The book of Revelation covers the time from the end of the apostolic age through the whole history of the church age and reaches into eternity. In the first two chapters of the book of Revelation, we find the seven churches in Asia. These churches were selected by the Lord with a specific reason because we know that towards the end of the first century, there were actually more than seven churches in the Roman province of Asia. There was the church at Colosse and others. The Holy Spirit purposely chose these seven churches because they represent the church of God throughout the ages. On the one hand, they were actually seven local assemblies in Asia at the time of the Apostle John; but they also prophetically tell us of the whole church history from the end of the apostolic age to the end of the church age.

These seven letters to the seven churches all end up with one call: "He that has an ear, let him hear what the Spirit says to the churches." This call is repeated seven times. I do believe that this is the call that has been going on throughout the whole church age; and this call is ringing out today in our midst: "He that has an ear, let him hear what the Spirit says to the churches." What is that call? What is the voice of the Spirit? We know that the call is the call to overcome. "He that overcomes", This is the call.

THE CALL TO OVERCOME

In order to know, to understand what the call really is, first of all, we need to know who the caller is. Who is calling us? The one who calls us is none other than our Lord Jesus. He is The Overcomer, and that is the reason why He calls us to overcome. He calls us to join with Him as overcomers. Here, our Lord Jesus reveals Himself, His fulness to His church. As He reveals His fulness to His church, He also examines His church in relation to His fulness to see whether they respond to His fulness, whether they correspond to what He is. After He examines, then you find the voice of the Holy Spirit. In other words, the Holy Spirit takes up that which our Lord Jesus is giving to us and cries out and says, "He that has an ear, let him hear what the Spirit says to the churches." We have the letters, we have the revelation, we have the examination and now we hear the voice of the Spirit saying, "Overcome."

OVERCOMERS IN EVERY AGE

Throughout this book of Revelation, we find this call to overcome ringing again and again. We do thank the Lord that there is not only that call to overcome but that throughout the church age, there have been, and there are, and there will be overcomers. In chapters 2 and 3 of the book of Revelation, in every letter, it says: "He that overcomes." There is not only that calling to overcome but there are actually those who overcome by the grace of God. These are the overcomers at the end of the apostolic age, at the end of the first century.

In chapter 7, you find countless number of people. They are standing there before the throne, clothed with white garments and waving palms in their hands. Who are they? They are the overcomers throughout the ages, from the second century to the end time. They are countless. In one sense, we do know that the overcomers are few. In every age, it seems to be that the overcomers are the minority, a remnant. And yet we do thank God, throughout the ages, there have been overcomers in every generation, in every age; and when they come together, you cannot count them. They are countless.

In chapter 12, you find the man child. The man child is a collective term. It represents the overcomers at the end time. We are in the end time; and there you find a man child is going to be born.

In chapter 15, there will be those who have overcome the beast and the mark of the beast. They will not worship the beast during that Great Tribulation time. They are there on the crystal sea before God. These are the overcomers through the Great Tribulation. Even out of the Great Tribulation, there will be overcomers.

When you come to chapter 17, you find that when our Lord Jesus comes down on earth for that final battle in the world of this present age, His army will be following Him. They are the "called, the chosen, the faithful." They are the overcomers of the church.

In chapter 20, you find thrones are set up, and those who sit upon the thrones are the overcomers of the ages. And in chapters 21 and 22, in New Jerusalem it says: "He that overcomes shall inherit these things, and I will be his God and he will be My son." Throughout the book of Revelation, there is the call to overcomers; and we do thank God that there are overcomers in every generation and in every age.

THE OVERCOMER

Our Lord Jesus is The Overcomer. From the time of Adam up to the time of our Lord Jesus, we do not see even one overcomer in the fullest sense. We find that Adam and the Adamic race have been and are defeated, captured by the enemy. But then, thank God, one day the Son of God came as a man; and as a man, He overcame. He overcame by His life, and He overcame by His death. In life, He overcame the enemy and all that is of the enemy in a personal way. In other words, He overcame as a person. When He was tempted, He overcame the tempter. When He was on earth, nothing could put Him under. He was always in charge, always in control. He was always above the circumstances. He was the only one who obeyed the Father, even unto death, and that the death of the cross. He was The Overcomer in life in a personal way. When He went to the cross at Calvary, He again overcame, but in a corporate way. In other words, He overcame not only for Himself, but He overcame for us. There on the cross, He laid the foundation for us to overcome. So in life and in death, our Lord Jesus overcame; and because He is The Overcomer, He is calling us to join Him as overcomers.

For all that has been begotten of God gets the victory over the world; and this is the victory which has gotten the victory over the world, our faith. Who is he that gets the victory over the world, but he that believes that Jesus is the Son of God? (1 John 5:4-5)

Who is he that gets the victory over the world? He who has been begotten of God; he who believes that Jesus is the Son of God. Dear brothers and sisters, are we those people? Are we not begotten of God? Do we not believe that Jesus is the Son of God? We do; and because we do, we have gotten the victory over the world, even our faith.

In the world, ye have tribulation, but be of good courage: (of good cheer) I have overcome the world. (John 16:33)

But in all these things we more than conquer through him that has loved us. (Romans 8:27)

But thanks be to God, who always leads us in triumph in the Christ. (2 Corinthians 2:14)

Our Lord Jesus is The Overcomer, and the church that He has redeemed is an overcoming church. The church is the church triumphant. The church is not supposed to be a defeated church; it is called to be an overcoming church. Every brother and sister in the church should be an overcomer because we have believed in the Lord Jesus; we have received His overcoming life. The whole church, as God has ordained her to be, is to be an overcoming church. Thank God for that.

THE FALLEN CHURCH

Unfortunately, we find that even at the close of the apostolic age, in the seven letters to the seven churches, when our Lord Jesus was walking in the midst of the seven lampstands and looking over these seven churches, what did He see? What did He find? He saw many things there, good and bad, but not of Him. He could hardly find Himself in some of these churches. Even at the end of the first century, they had lost their first love. The work was going on, the labor was going on; but the inward reality, that inward power and force, was gone. They had lost their first love. False teachings had begun to slip into the church. Corrupt manners had begun to find their way into the church. The church had fallen from what it ought to be. Instead of being overcomers, the church had fallen and had been defeated.

OVERCOMERS OF THE CHURCH

Even in the first century, at the end of the apostolic age, the church had already failed in her calling. They were not what He was; and because of that, there is the calling to overcome: "He that overcomes." To every local assembly at that time, the Spirit of God was calling out to each one personally. The church as a whole had fallen, but now the calling comes to each one personally: "He that overcomes." Who is he that overcomes? It is he who responds to the revelation of Christ. In every church, He tells us who He is; He reveals Himself to us. And His revelation ought to be our vocation so that we respond to what has been revealed to us. But here you find many did not respond. But those who responded to Christ, to His fulness, were the overcomers.

The overcomers of the church are not super Christians. The overcomers of the church are normal Christians because Christians have become abnormal, subnormal. This is the reason why those who respond to the revelation of Jesus Christ, those who respond to the fulness of

Christ are the normal Christians, and they are the overcomers. They are those who are to stand for the whole church. They are to do the work of the whole church. They are to bear the testimony of Jesus for the whole church because the testimony of God cannot fail. He will have His testimony in every generation and every century. So here you find the call to overcome, and this call has been going out for two thousand years. And we do believe that today this call is upon us. Dear brothers and sisters, the whole church ought to be an overcoming church; but if the whole has failed, then God is calling for overcomers of the church.

THE END TIME

Chapter 12 of the book of Revelation tells us of the overcomers at the end time. Now brothers and sisters, we all know that we are in the end time, the last days. What is the end time? What is the last days? The last days or the end time is a term we find when we read the Scriptures, and you can even find it in the Old Testament. It refers to the time that our Lord Jesus came to this earth. So in other words, the last days actually began with the first coming of our Lord Jesus, and it will end with His second coming. The whole time is the last days. In the letter of the apostles, it is mentioned that these are the last days. So actually, the last days or the end time refers to the time from the first coming of the Lord Jesus to the second coming of the Lord Jesus. If this is the case, then we are at the end of the end time.We are at the last of the last days. This is a very critical time. We know that the Lord is coming soon. We know that this is the end of the end time; and we are living in a very, very vital, important period. This is the time that we are involved in, and that is the reason why we should pay special attention to this chapter.

WOMAN REPRESENTS THE CHURCH

John saw a woman in travail, in pain. Who is that woman? Without going into detailed interpretation or into many interpretations, we will just mention it very briefly. In the Scripture, God often uses woman to represent the church. Eve, in the garden of Eden, is a type of the church. Adam represents Christ, he is a type of

Christ. Eve represents the church in God's original thought. We find in Ephesians 5, that Christ loved the church and gave Himself for her. He purified it, sanctified it, by the washing of the water with the word, that He might present to Himself a glorious church, without spot or wrinkle or any such thing, holy and blameless. That woman represents the church through the church age. Throughout the church age, our Lord Jesus isnourishing and cherishing His body in order to bring that body to maturity, that she may become His bride. In Revelation 12, there is a woman, and that woman again represents the church. But it is the church at the end of the end time. There, she is in travail, in pain for birth. In Revelation 21 and 22, you find another woman, the holy city, the New Jerusalem. She is the bride, the Lamb's wife, and that is the church in eternity. So, you find that woman represents the church.

THE TRAVAILING OF OUR LORD JESUS

This woman in Revelation 12 is in travail; she is in birth pains. She is going to bring forth a child. Brothers and sisters, is it not a universal law that if there is no travail, there is no birth? If you are looking for a birth, you have to suffer and to travail in pain in order to bring it forth. This is true physically, and this is true spiritually.

In Isaiah 53, it is said of our Lord Jesus that He shall see the fruit of the travail of His soul and be satisfied. Our Lord Jesus travailed in His soul, especially in the garden of Gethsemane. That does not mean He did not travail before that. As a matter of fact, He was the Lamb slain from the foundation of the world. His very incarnation was a travail. His whole life on earth was a travail. But we find especially in the garden of Gethsemane, how He travailed. There He said He was sorrowful even to death. He was deeply distressed, agonizing. He asked His three disciples who were closest to Him to wait with Him, and He went forward. He prayed, "Father, if it be possible, let this cup be passed from Me, but not My will, Thy will be done." As He travailed in prayer, the Bible says His sweat came out like blood drops; and the angel had to appear and sustain Him. In other words, if the angel had not sustained Him, He might have died in the garden of Gethsemane. The conflict was tremendous. We could never understand what transpired in the garden of Gethsemane. Our Lord Jesus travailed there in prayer; He was to give birth. On the cross, He cried out, "My God, My God why has Thou forsaken Me?" What a travail! Unbearable.

When people were crucified, usually they did not die in several hours; they might linger for days. The two robbers who were crucified with Him were still alive. They had to have their legs broken to speed them to death. But when the soldier came to our Lord Jesus, He was already dead. To make sure that He was dead, a soldier thrust a spear through His side. It entered into His very heart, and out of Him came blood and water. John witnessed it, and he said, "What I saw was true." He said it very emphatically. Why? Brothers and sisters, out of the side of our Lord Jesus, God took something to build a woman. The church is built with His blood, with His life: blood to atone our sins, water represents His life to give us life. We are the fruit of the travail of His soul; and when He sees us,

He is satisfied. It is just like a woman when she is in travail.She is in pain, and probably, she goes through a sense of death. But after a child is born, she forgets all her sorrows; she rejoices. And this is our Lord Jesus; He rejoices in His church.

THE TRAVAILING OF THOSE WITH CHRIST'S HEART

Not only does our Lord Jesus travail, but we are called to the fellowship of His suffering.

My children, of whom I again travail in birth until Christ shall have been formed in you. (Galatians 4:19)

Brothers and sisters, oh how those who know the heart of our Lord Jesus, those who love the church as Christ loved the church travail for us that Christ may be formed in us. Many brothers and sisters remain as babes and do not grow up. Many brothers and sisters are deformed. Those who have the burden of Christ and have known the heart of Christ for the church, who love the church, travail; they travail in prayer. They agonize that Christ may be formed, fully formed in us; that we may be made full, that we may know the fulness of Christ. That is the travail going on.

THE TRAVAILING OF THE WORLD

As a matter of fact, the whole world is travailing. In Romans 8, we are told that the whole world, all creation, is groaning together. It is travailing in pain together. It is waiting for the manifestation of the sons of God that it might be set free from the corruption, the vanity it has been put in by man. Do you know it is man who has put the whole creation into bondage, into corruption? The creation is innocent; we are the guilty ones. But all creation groans. If you have ears to hear, you can hear the groaning of all creation. It is longing for liberty, to be set free from the bondage, from emptiness. When will it be set free? When the sons of God are manifested; when the church becomes a full grown man, and comes unto the measure of the stature of the fulness of Christ; when the man child is born. Then the whole creation will be liberated from corruption and bondage.

MATURING THROUGH PRESSURES

Paul says in Romans 8, that even we, the first fruits of the Spirit, groan in ourselves, waiting for adoption, for the redemption of our body. Brothers and sisters, is it not true that we do groan within ourselves? Especially as we come to the last time, the pressure increases to a tremendous degree. Believers, today, are under great pressure. Probably, our forefathers never experienced such pressure as we are in today. The world is pressing upon us. The enemy is tempting us, deceiving us, attacking us, trying to devour and kill us. We are pressed from all sides. We are pressed by the world situation; we are pressed by the political situation; by the economic situation; we are pressed by the social situation; we are pressed by the moral situation of the world; we are pressed in the family; we are pressed in the work. The pressure is tremendous today. The enemy wants to break us. Brothers and sisters, when we are under such pressure, are we groaning? Are we travailing? Do we give ourselves to prayer?

There is not only the pressure around us, but we find the Spirit of God groans within us. The pressure around us is to crush us; but the Holy Spirit groans within us that we may grow, we may be matured, we may expand, and we may rise above. In pressure, we are enlarged. This is the growing pains. This is the way that we grow into the fulness of Christ. If we allow these pressures to crush us, we miss the point. These pressures that come upon us serve as a kind of opportunity. The Holy Spirit within us groans for birth, groans for growth; and if we give ourselves to Christ, if we yield ourselves, if we cooperate with the Holy Spirit, all these pressures will only mature us.All these sufferings will only bring us into conformity to the image of Christ. Do we travail within? Are we benefited by the travailing?

THE TRAVAILING FOR THE MAN CHILD

That woman in chapter 12 is in travail, in pain, but unfortunately, she does not enter into the real meaning of travailing. Why? The red dragon, Satan, is standing before that woman.

We know that Satan is opposing Christ because when Christ was on earth, he was trying to kill Him. When He was born, Herod tried to kill all the children in Bethlehem below two years of age. When our Lord Jesus came out to minister in His own city of Nazareth, they pushed Him out of the synagogue onto the cliff and tried to push Him down and kill Him.Satan tried to kill our Lord Jesus. Finally, he succeeded in killing Him on the cross; but he found that he was killed.

Throughout the church age, that dragon has been trying to devour the church, to kill the church by taking away the first love: "You may continue on outwardly, but there is no reality in it." When he could not succeed in doing that, then he tried to do it outwardly by persecuting the church and trying to wipe it out; but he could not do it. But sadly, you find at this time, the dragon is standing before the woman, but he has no interest in the woman. In other words, he is saying: "You can exist. You do not count to me. My kingdom will not suffer because of you. You have lost the reality; you have lost the power; you have lost the testimony." The dragon does not care about that woman; he cares about that man child in the womb. Through the travailing, there is a man child growing into maturity within the womb of that woman, and the enemy knows that man child will be his end. He is waiting for that man child to come out, and then he will devour him.

Brothers and sisters, isn't that a picture of today? When we look at the church today, what do we see? In spite of all the pressure, in spite of all the things that are happening, it seems that the church does not respond to the working of the Spirit within. It seems as if the church is not groaning. It seems as if the church is like the church in Laodicea. They are boasting: Look, we have become so big, so influential, so prosperous. We lack nothing. Isn't that the picture of the church today? If you want to know what the church is, see what the attitude of the red dragon is. He may stand before that woman and will not even bother to do anything with her. She does not count. The church today does not count, not in the sight of God, nor even in the sight of the enemy.The church has fallen. The

Scripture says there will be a falling away, the apostasy, a general falling away of the church.

But thank God, within the womb of the church, a man child is growing. These people receive the benefit of all the pressures and the movement of the Holy Spirit within. They respond to the voice of the Spirit. They repent; they return; they go back to the source; they humble themselves; they empty themselves; they deny themselves; they look at the Lord; they receive from Him what He is. Brothers and sisters, these are the people the enemy is afraid of.

This man child is collective because we are told "They overcome." In these last days, the Spirit of God is calling for overcomers. He does not call you to be super Christians; He calls you to be normal Christians. He calls you to respond to the revelation of Jesus Christ. He calls you to receive Christ Jesus in all His fulness. He calls you to be faithful to Him. He calls you to bear His testimony in these last days. Will you respond?

THE RAPTURE OF THE MAN CHILD

When this man child is born, do you think the enemy can devour him? Actually, in the womb of the woman, he has already defeated the enemy. He has got the victory. The Lord has led him in triumph. As soon as he is born, he is caught up, raptured, to the throne of God. This rapture is the sign of the coming of the Lord: the parousia, the presence of the Lord. One day, brothers and sisters, when the world says, "Peace, peace," when the world is sleeping, suddenly, throughout the whole world, a number of the Lord's children will disappear. The Lord will take them to the throne. As they are taken to the throne, they go through the air, the headquarters of Satan. They break through the headquarters of the enemy, and they arrive at the throne where The Overcomer is. Because of this, the Bible says there will be war in the air. Michael and his angels will fight with Satan and his angels, and Satan will be defeated and thrown from the air to the earth with his angels. The air must be cleared for Christ to descend. Be delightful, those who are in heaven; but woe to those who are on earth because Satan now is on earth (see Revelation 12:12). He knows his time is very short.

THE BLOOD OF THE LAMB

This man child, these overcomers are not super Christians. They do not overcome because of themselves. They overcome because of the blood of the Lamb. They are not perfect; they are weak; they may even fall. But they know the preciousness of the blood of the Lamb. Whenever they fall, they repent. They go to the blood of the Lamb and have their garments washed. Satan is the accuser. Sometimes, his accusation has some ground, unfortunately; but many times, he exaggerates, and it is completely false. We do thank God, that we have the blood of the Lamb, and that blood shuts up his mouth. The nearer we are to the Lord, the more precious we find the blood. Do not think that you can outgrow the blood of the Lamb. Brothers and sisters, the closer we are to the Lord, the more we know how weak we are; how full of spot, wrinkle and blemish we are. How we need the blood to wash us day by day, hour by hour. Even our tears of repentance need to be washed by the blood. Thank God for the blood of the Lamb!

Oftentimes, the enemy tries to use darkness to surround us. We do not even know ourselves; and therefore, we may have sinned and not know it. Or we may not have sinned, but we are in darkness, under accusation, and we think we have sinned. But if we walk in the light as God is in the light, we shall have fellowship one with another; and the blood of Jesus, God's Son, shall wash us, cleanse us from all our sins. We have this light of life we have received from the Lord Jesus shining within us; and if we walk in that light as He is in the light, we will have fellowship with Him, and the blood of Jesus will wash us from all our sins. In other words, there is no need for us to be in darkness; there is no need for us to be in defilement; there is no need for us to be under accusation; there is no need for us to have our fellowship, communion with God interrupted. These people have uninterrupted communion with God. That is the secret to overcoming, and it is based on the blood of the Lamb.

THE WORD OF THEIR TESTIMONY

They overcame because of the word of their testimony. What is their testimony? They have a testimony; but as Paul says, "I do not preach myself, I preach Christ." Our testimony is not ourselves; our testimony is the testimony of Jesus. What is the testimony of Jesus? To put it in one word, the testimony of Jesus is: I am the first and the last and the living One. I have become dead, and I am living and live forevermore; and I hold in My hands the keys of death and Hades. This is the testimony of Jesus. These people know the fulness of Christ. They know that Christ is the first. He has to be the first in all things in their lives. They know that Christ is the last. He has to have the last word in their lives. They know that Christ is the living One; He is life. He is not only the One who died for us but He is our life. They know His life. They know that Christ has died, but He is resurrected. In other words, they know the cross. The cross is not a theory to them. And they know resurrection life. They know that Christ has in His hands the keys of death and Hades. They know the victory of Christ. This is their testimony.

They have the word of testimony, and they speak out. When they say, "Jesus is Lord," there is power in their word because they have a life to back it up. Sometimes we say it, but there is no power because there is no testimony behind it. Oh, brothers and sisters, may we know Christ. To know Him, and to know the power of His resurrection; to have fellowship with His suffering; to be conformed to His death, this is our testimony, the word of our testimony. And when we say, "Jesus is Lord," Satan flees.

THEY LOVE NOT THEIR LIVES UNTO DEATH

They loved not their lives even unto death. That is their attitude. The life there is the soul life. The Lord Jesus said: "If anyone will come after Me, let him deny himself, take up his cross and follow Me. He who loves his life shall lose it, but he who hates his life and loses his life for My sake, and for the gospel's sake, shall gain it to eternity" (see Mark 8:34-35). We all have that soul life, self, in us. Do we deny ourselves, take up the cross and follow the Lord? Wherever the Lamb goes, we go. These are the overcomers.

They shall shepherd the nations with an iron rod. They shall reign with Christ for a thousand years. They are the ones who prepare the way for the return of our Lord Jesus; and they are the ones doing the work for the whole church. May God have mercy upon us.

Dear Heavenly Father, how we praise and thank Thee that Thou art working out Thy purpose. We pray, Lord, that all the sufferings that go on in this world to Thy church, to us individually, may not be in vain; but they will bring forth that which answers to Thy heart. We pray that by Thy grace we may be among those who overcome, not for ourselves; it is for the church; it is for Thee. We ask in Thy precious name. Amen.

FULNESS IN RELATION TO NEW JERUSALEM

Revelation 21:1-7 And I saw a new heaven and a new earth; for the first heaven and the first earth had passed away, and the sea exists no more.

And I saw the holy city, new Jerusalem, coming down out of the heaven from God, prepared as a bride adorned for her husband.And I heard a loud voice out of the heaven, saying, Behold, the tabernacle of God is with men, and he shall tabernacle with them, and they shall be his people, and God himself shall be with them, their God. And he shall wipe away every tear from their eyes; and death shall not exist anymore, nor grief, nor cry, nor distress shall exist anymore, for the former things have passed away. And he that sat on the throne said, Behold, I make all things new. And he says to me, Write, for these words are true and faithful. And he said to me, It is done. I am the Alpha and the Omega, the beginning and the end. I will give to him that thirsts of the fountain of the water of life freely. He that overcomes shall inherit these things, and I will be to him God.

Revelation 22:20 He that testifies these things says, Yea, I come quickly. Amen; come, Lord Jesus.

Lord, as we come to the last session of the ministry of Thy Word, we do acknowledge Thee as the end, as Thou art the beginning. We just commit this time into Thy hands and ask Thee again to open our eyes that we may see what Thy servant John saw. We pray that our hearts will really be touched by Thee and be drawn to Thee that we may cry out, "Come, Lord Jesus." In the name of our Lord Jesus. Amen.

We have been looking at the fulness of Christ in the book of Revelation. At the end of the last book of the Bible, we see the consummation of all things. We see the fulness of Christ manifested in all things. Even before the foundation of the world, in eternity past, God made a will according to His good pleasure. He wants His Son to have the first place in all things; that is to say, He wants all things to manifest the glory of His Beloved. He wants the fulness of Himself that is located in His Son to fill all things.

Then He began to work in time. Even though during the period called "time" it seems as if His plan has been frustrated from time to time, we do thank God that He continues to work until, one day, His will will be fully realized.

In the fulness of time, God sent His beloved Son into the world. When His Son was crucified on the cross, before He gave up His Spirit to the Father, He shouted with a loud shout, "It is finished." The work of redemption is finished. He has laid the foundation for the restoration of all things. He has reconciled all things by the blood of the cross to His fulness, and after that, it is just a development of that which has been laid. In Revelation 21, God declares: "Behold, I make all things new... It is done." The word It is done actually means "they are fulfilled." The Apostle John saw the old heaven and the old earth had burned and passed away. There will be a new heaven and a new earth. He saw the holy city, new Jerusalem, descending from God above upon this earth. This city, new Jerusalem, is the manifestation of the fulness of Christ in a corporate way.

JOHN'S REACTION TO THE VISION

We want to see that vision the Apostle John saw almost two thousand years ago. When John saw the new Jerusalem, the tabernacle of God, coming to man, you know what he did? The news was so good, tremendous, that he fell down and worshipped the messenger. Of course, the angel said, No, don't do that; we are fellow servants; worship God.

In this book of Revelation, I think it is very interesting if you notice the reaction of John. Sometimes, John wept; and here, you find he did a most foolish thing, as it were. John knew the Lord so well. He knew God so well, and yet, somehow, when he saw that vision of new Jerusalem, it touched his heart so much he forgot; he worshipped the angel. And he was forbidden to do that. Now you must understand the feeling of John at that moment; and if you understand his feeling, probably, you will not blame him. Brothers and sisters, do we have the same reaction? If we see new Jerusalem, if we see what God has done, we will really be beside ourselves. We will not know what to do, and we will really worship God. What a God we have! What He has done for us!

JERUSALEM ON EARTH

The holy city, the new Jerusalem, is the corporate expression of the fulness of Christ. Truly, it is that body that is filled with the fulness of Christ. Now in order to know this new Jerusalem, probably, it will be good for us to know what Jerusalem is. We are all familiar with the name Jerusalem; it is a city of peace. It is a city on earth where God put His name. It is a city in which there is the throne of David. It is a city in which there is the temple of Solomon. In that city, God dwells; in that city, He rules; in that city, He is served and worshipped. The Psalmist says the twelve tribes will go to that city as a testimony of the oneness of God's people. Out of that city, the law goes forth. All the nations will come and bring their tribute to it. This is Jerusalem on earth.

The first mentioning of Jerusalem is found in Genesis 14. When Abraham defeated the four kings and rescued Lot, as he was coming back from victory, he was met by a king, Melchisedec, king of Salem. It was really a very strange thing. The Canaanites represent the evil forces in this world, and they occupied the land of Canaan. But in the midst of these seven tribes of the Canaanites, there was the city of Salem, a city of peace. And there was a king in that city, Melchisedec, the king of righteousness. He came to meet Abraham, and he gave him wine and bread, and he blessed Abraham. That is the first mentioning of the city of Salem, Jerusalem.

Later on, this city was occupied by the Jebusites. In 2 Samuel, when David became king, the first thing he did was to take Jerusalem out of the hands of the Jebusites and make it the capital. Evidently, by revelation, he knew that this was the place where God had chosen to put His name. So he set his throne there. Then Solomon, his son, built the temple there.

After the nation of Israel was divided into the northern kingdom of Israel and the southern kingdom of Judah, Jerusalem remained as the capital of the southern kingdom for about five hundred years. Then it was destroyed by the

Babylonian army, and the people of God were taken into Babylonian captivity.

Even though it is the city of peace, this city has known more turmoil, confusion, and war than any other city in the world. This city has been occupied by many nations. In the book of Isaiah, chapter 2, we find that at the end of the days, the mountain of God's house will be lifted up and all nations will flow into it. This is Jerusalem.

CORPORATE EXPRESSION OF THE FULNESS OF CHRIST

However, even this Jerusalem will pass away; because when the old earth passes away, Jerusalem on earth will also pass away. But what God is really after is what Jerusalem on earth represents. What God is really after is that new Jerusalem. In other words, all that Jerusalem represents will be realized fully in new Jerusalem. That new Jerusalem is not earthly; it is heavenly. It descends from heaven upon the new earth. This new Jerusalem is not physical; it is spiritual. Can you imagine a city as a wife?

Surely this should tell us that what God desires to show us is the principles, the spiritual reality, not a literal city.New Jerusalem is a city, but it is not a literal city. How can a city become a wife? But we find that all the characteristics, the spiritual principles, are being manifested in this new Jerusalem. It is just like when we say our Lord Jesus is the Lamb of God. He is a Lamb, but is He literally a lamb? Of course not! He is the Lamb of God because He has the spirit, the character of a lamb. This is the same thing with that holy city, the new Jerusalem. It is the final, corporate expression of the fulness of Christ. The foundation that Christ has laid on Calvary's cross and God has built is finalized in that city.

As a matter of fact, even Abraham looked forward to that city. In Hebrews 11, it says Abraham was a pilgrim, a stranger, a sojourner in the Promise Land. If he had wanted to return to his own home in Ur of Chaldea, he could have done that. But he was looking forward to a city with foundations built by God Himself. All the saints in the Old Testament time and all the saints in the New Testament time are looking forward to that city, the holy city, the new

Jerusalem that God has built; and it will be the fulness of Christ in a corporate way.

CHARACTERISTICS OF NEW JERUSALEM

A City of Unity

First of all, this new Jerusalem is a city, and a city speaks to us of unity. A city is an aggregate of people; many but one. There are many people, but they live together as one unit, under one government, under one rule, under one administration. This is what a city is.

There is a goal before us, and that goal is: "Until we all arrive at the unity of the faith and of the knowledge of the Son of God, at the full-grown man..." (Ephesians 4:13). Here you are. This new Jerusalem is a city. It is the unity of the faith and of the full knowledge of the Son of God. It is made of many people, but they are one. They are one under one government, and that government is upon the shoulder of our Lord Jesus. There, He is the Head; He is the Lord, unchallenged, fully submitted to. One day, this will become a reality.

A Bride

This is not only a city, this is a bride, the Lamb's wife. When we think of wife, bride, it tells us of union; it tells us of growth; it tells us of love. You cannot have a wife who is a baby. She has to be full-grown. We are the body of Christ today, and how our Lord Jesus loves His body. No one hates his body; and here our Lord Jesus loves His body. He sanctifies it, purifies it with the washing of the water by the Word in order to present that body to Himself, a glorious church without spot or wrinkle or any of such thing, holy and blameless. Brothers and sisters this body is growing. It is growing into maturity, unto a full-grown man; and when it has become a full-grown man, then our Lord will return and take her to be His bride. There will be that eternal union, and there will be that everlasting love, "Unto a full-grown man."

The Tabernacle of God

Again, you find this city is not only the Lamb's wife, it is also the tabernacle of God among man. Brothers and sisters, it is the eternal purpose of God, eternal wish of God to dwell among His own. He created man in His own image; He gives him the capacity to receive God that God may dwell in him and among man.

After He redeemed the children of Israel out of Egypt, He revealed to them His purpose in delivering them. God did not deliver the children of Israel out of Egypt just that they might be free to do anything they wanted to do. God delivered the children of Israel out of Egypt with a very specific reason, but He did not reveal that reason until He took them to the Mount of Sinai. There He revealed that He wanted to dwell among them, and He asked them to build a tabernacle for Him that He might live among His people. Later on, you find David, who loved God very much, who knew God's heart, desired to build a permanent house for God.God was pleased, and his son Solomon built the temple. When the tabernacle was erected, the glory of God came and filled it. When the temple was built the glory of God again came and filled it. God took up His abode among His people. That has been God's desire throughout the ages. But the temple was destroyed.

The Son of God came into this world. He was the real temple of God, and the glory of God rested on Him. We contemplated His glory, even as the glory of the only begotten with the Father. But that glory was veiled because He came in the flesh. The glory was there within, but it was veiled. People did not see it; only those with spiritual eyes could see it. Throughout His life on earth, only once did that glory break out, and it was on the Mount of Transfiguration. But did the glory of God ever depart from that temple? It did. When our Lord Jesus cried out, "My God, My God, why has Thou forsaken Me?" the glory departed. There was darkness upon this earth because God's beloved Son was made a sin offering for the world.

But thank God, now our Lord Jesus is crowned with glory and honor, and He has returned to His glory. He poured down His Spirit on the day of Pentecost, and glory filled that spiritual temple. On the day of Pentecost one hundred and twenty people were baptized in one Spirit into one body; and the glory of God, in the Spirit, filled that body. Unfortunately, we find how the church has failed. But thank God, that day is coming when He shall have His tabernacle, filled with glory, and it will never depart. God will dwell among man; and His purpose will be fulfilled.

A City That Shines With the Glory of God

An angel said to John: "Do you want to have a closer look at that new Jerusalem? I will show you." The angel took him, in the spirit, to a high mountain; and he saw that city full of glory. It has the shining of the glory of God.

What is glory? Many people have tried to explain and define it, but whatever definition we may try, it really confines and limits what glory is. Glory is undefinable. Glory is what God is; glory is the sum total of the character of God; glory is His presence and His satisfaction. This city is shining with the glory of God. In other words, it is a glorious church without spot or wrinkle or any of such thing. This city is so transparent that the glory of God can shine through it without distortion, without discount. To put it in another way: it is full of glory, full of God, and nothing else.

As John looked at this city, he found the shining like a most precious stone, as a crystal-like jasper stone. We first read of jasper stone in chapter 4 of the book of Revelation. When John was taken in spirit to heaven, he saw a throne, and One sitting upon the throne with the appearance of jasper and sardius. So jasper here represents the character, the nature of God. The shining is like a most precious stone, as a crystal-like jasper stone. In other words, this city has taken up the nature and character of God; it is crystal-like.It shines through without any interruption. It is all of God and nothing else.

A Perfect City

Then John saw this city. Actually, this city is a cube because the length and the width and the height are all equal. An angel measured it with a golden reed; and the measurement of the width and the length and the height is twelve thousand stadia, which is approximately fifteen hundred miles. Can you think of a city fifteen hundred miles up, fifteen hundred miles wide, and fifteen hundred miles long? It would be from New York to Miami. And not only the width and the length but the height is twelve thousand stadia. It is the multiple of twelve, and twelve in the Scripture speaks of perfection. It is perfect measurement, up to the full measure. "Unto the measure of the stature of the fulness of Christ.

A HOLY CITY

The wall is one hundred and forty-four cubits, roughly two hundred feet. Again, it is a multiple of twelve. This whole city is just perfect. We will be like Him, as He is, by the grace of God. Grace will do that. And the wall is made of jasper. We mentioned already that jasper represents the nature, the character of God. What is a wall for? Wall in the Scripture is very important. The problem, in the beginning of human history, was a problem of walls. There was a garden, but there was no wall. Actually, God wanted Adam to be that wall, but Adam failed. So the enemy crept in, tempted man and man fell. There was no wall. Wall is separation; wall is protection. A wall walls in all that is within it, and it excludes all that is without it.

Wall is very important in the Scripture. In the recovery of Jerusalem, the wall had to be built up. Even though the temple was rebuilt, without a wall it was not finished. But here you find a finished product, the wall, and the wall is one hundred and forty-four cubits. We have never seen a wall that high. It is a perfect separation. And that wall is made of jasper. In other words, it is the very life of God that makes the separation. It is the full life of God, the full separation, and we know separation is but another word for holiness. This is a holy city. This is a city that is separated from all that is not of God, and it includes all that is of God; it is well protected.

What is holiness? We are supposed to be a holy nation, a holy people. We are supposed to be separated from the world, separated from anything that is not of God; but how are we separated? Are we separated by keeping some rules and regulations? No; we are separated by the life of God. The reason God's people are not holy, are not separated as we should be, is not because we do not have enough rules and regulations; it is because we are lacking in life.

As we grow in the life of God in Christ Jesus, it naturally separates us from all that is not of God. It will separate us from the world, from self, from sin, from the enemy, and from anything that is not of God; and it will keep us in all that is of God. Ephesians 1 says that God wants us to be holy and blameless before Him in love; this is the will of God. So here you find holiness is completed. This is the holy city.

A City With a Foundation of Christ

There are twelve foundations with twelve precious stones bearing the names of the twelve apostles. Now we all know that this city with foundations that God built has only one foundation. The Apostle Paul tells us there is no other foundation but the foundation that has been laid which is Christ Jesus. The Lord Jesus, Himself, declared: "I will build My church upon this rock and the gates of Hades shall not prevail against it" (Matthew 16:18). In other words, He is the Rock, He is the foundation of that holy city, the new Jerusalem.

Yet you find the Scripture says there are twelve foundations of twelve precious stones. Even in Ephesians 2, it is said that the apostles and the prophets are the foundation of that habitation of God. Is there any contradiction? No; because these twelve precious stones, even though they are all distinct and different, one represents Peter, one represents John, one represents James, there is still that individuality there. You can recognize these different stones. They are not just one kind of precious stone but they are all different precious stones. They all have a different color and a different brilliancy. Yet, even though they are all different, they are just varieties of Christ. In other words, the apostles do not have their teaching; the teaching of the apostles is none other than the teaching of Christ. The apostles have no other fellowship but the fellowship of Christ. It is through the prophets and the apostles that Christ is made known to us, and that is the reason why the foundations are the foundations of the prophets and the teachers. But, in actuality, it is Christ. Outwardly, you see Peter; but actually, it is Christ in Peter.

A City With Gates of Pearl

The gates are made of pearls. Pearl speaks of the work of the Holy Spirit, how the Holy Spirit works very patiently in us in order to bring us to Christ. It bears the name of the twelve tribes of Israel because salvation comes from the Jews. You have the shining of the glory of God. You have the foundation of the work of Christ Jesus. You have the gates of the pearls of the operation of the Holy Spirit. The triune God has done the work and produced this holy city, new Jerusalem.

A City of Pure Gold

Look a little closer, and you find this city is made of gold. When Solomon built the temple, he overlaid it with gold. But here you find the whole city is pure gold, transparent gold. It is not just overlaid with gold. We have never seen such gold. Gold represents, again, the nature of God. So you find this whole city is built with God's own nature. There is nothing of wood or straw. It is all of God, and it is transparent.

A City With One Street

There is only one street there. People try to figure out, with that huge city and twelve gates, how it can be that there is only one street. Some people have come up with the idea of a spiral that goes around and around and around and around until it reaches the top where the throne of God and the Lamb is. But anyway, there is only one street, and the street is of gold. We often sing the song that we will walk on the street of gold. I do not know if you will really like it because that gold is transparent.

Street in the Scripture speaks of fellowship. You walk on the street; you go and come on the street. It is the fellowship of all the saints. We have only one fellowship, one street. Today, you have many bypasses; but in new Jerusalem, there is no bypass, only one street. Today, you find this fellowship and that fellowship. We want to fellowship with these people, but we do not want to fellowship with that people. But in that day, there is only one fellowship. It is the fellowship of God's Son; it is the fellowship in the Spirit; it is the fellowship of the saints. There is one fellowship; and all fellowship leads to the throne, and it all comes from the throne.

What is fellowship? Oftentimes, we think gossip is fellowship. But it does not lead us to the throne; neither does it come forth from the throne. Through fellowship, we are led to God, to Christ. Fellowship comes from God, from Christ. We fellowship Christ; and the more we fellowship, the more we draw nigh to that throne.

That fellowship is really open fellowship. There is no hiding because the gold is transparent. Everything in you is visible, every thought is visible, every word is heard. There is no hiding; it is open fellowship. Brothers and sisters, how we long for that day. Today, when we fellowship with one another, we try to cover up something. We have to. There is still not that open fellowship. It will be wonderful when that day comes when there is no hiding, when we are transparent to one another.

The River of Life, The Tree of Life

Strangely, there is not only just one street, there is only one river. There is a river of life that flows out from the throne of God, and this river goes through the whole city. But I do not know whether that river is in the midst of the street. Then you will find the tree of life, just one tree. But that one tree covers the whole city on this side and that side of the street; and that tree produces twelve fruits, one in each season. Of course, we know that river of life signifies the Holy Spirit. The Holy Spirit, the fulness of the Spirit, flows through the whole city, and it produces the fruit of life according to season, according to needs. There is no lacking.

The Center of the City is the Throne

The center of that city is the throne, the throne of God and of the Lamb. All who are in that city are kings. They have the name of God upon their forehead, and they serve God.

Brothers and sisters, this is the picture of eternity to come. This is the picture when God's will is fully realized. This is the picture of the fulness of Christ manifested in a corporate way. This is what God is doing. This is what the Spirit of God is working in each one of us until we arrive, until God has what He wants, until the Son has His bride. Is it a dream? No; it is real. With man, it is impossible; but with God, all things are possible. He is doing it; He will do it. He who calls us is faithful; He will perform it.

But brothers and sisters, when we are given such a vision of what, eventually, finally, God will possess, is our heart stirred just like John's was?Are we really attracted by what we see? Are we now willing to give up everything for that? Are we willing to cooperate with the Holy Spirit? Are we willing to deny ourselves, take up the cross and follow Him? Because this is the goal; this is what, by the grace of God, we will arrive at for God, and for ourselves. This ought to lead us to worship. What a God we have! How good, how precious are His thoughts toward us; what He has done for us in Christ Jesus; what He is laboring, by His Spirit, patiently with us, even now. May we always have that vision before us, and may we be a worshipping people.

Shall we pray:

Dear Heavenly Father, our God, we worship Thee. What Thou has willed is beyond our thinking, our comprehension; but we know that Thou has purposed, in Thy beloved Son, such a tremendous, glorious purpose.Oh, how we praise and thank Thee the day is coming when the glory of God shall fill the universe, when the fulness of Christ shall fill all things. Praise and thank God that Thou has called us with such a high calling. Oh, our cry unto Thee is: May that day come. Come, Lord Jesus. Amen.

Other Books Printed By
Christian Testimony Ministry

SPEAKER	TITLE
DANA CONGDON	MARRIAGE, SINGLENESS, AND THE WILL OF GOD
	RECOVERY & RESTORATION
	THE HOLY SPIRIT
	HEBREWS
A.J. FLACK	TENT OF HIS SPLENDOUR
STEPHEN KAUNG	ACTS
	BE YE THEREFORE PERFECT
	CALLED OUT UNTO CHRIST
	CALLED TO THE FELLOWSHIP OF GOD'S SON
	DIVINE LIFE AND ORDER
	FOR ME TO LIVE IS CHRIST
	GLORIOUS LIBERTY OF THE CHILDREN OF GOD
	GOD'S PURPOSE FOR THE FAMILY
	I WILL BUILD MY CHURCH
	MEDITATIONS ON THE KINGDOM
	RECOVERY
	SPIRITUAL EXERCISE
	SPIRITUAL LIFE (II CORINTHIANS SERIES)
	TEACH US TO PRAY
	THE CROSS
	THE FULNESS OF CHRIST—IN THE BOOK OF REVELATION
	THE HEADSHIP OF CHRIST
	THE KINGDOM AND THE CHURCH
	THE KINGDOM OF GOD
	THE LAST CALL TO THE CHURCHES, THE CALL TO OVERCOME
	THE LIFE OF OUR LORD JESUS
	THE LIFE OF THE CHURCH, THE BODY OF CHRIST
	THE LORD'S TABLE
	TWO GUIDEPOSTS FOR INHERITING THE KINGDOM
	VISION OF CHRIST (REVELATION)
	WHO ARE WE?

WHY DO WE SO GATHER?
WORSHIP

LANCE LAMBERT   CALLED UNTO HIS ETERNAL GLORY
GOD'S ETERNAL PURPOSE
IN THE DAY OF THY POWER
JACOB I HAVE LOVED
LIVING FAITH
LESSONS FROM THE LIFE OF MOSES
LOVE DIVINE
MY HOUSE SHALL BE A HOUSE OF PRAYER
PREPARATION FOR THE COMING OF THE LORD
REIGNING WITH CHRIST
SPIRITUAL CHARACTER
THE GOSPEL OF THE KINGDOM
THE IMPORTANCE OF COVERING
THE LAST DAYS AND GOD'S PRIORITIES
THE PRIZE
THE SUPREMACY OF JESUS CHRIST
THINE IS THE POWER!
THOU ART MINE

T. AUSTIN-SPARKS   THE LORD'S TESTIMONY AND THE WORLD NEED

HARVEY CEDARS CONFERENCE

STEPHEN KAUNG   HEAVENLY VISION
SPIRITUAL RESPONSIBILITY

CONGDON, HILE, KAUNG   SPIRITUAL MINISTRY
SPIRITUAL AUTHORITY
SPIRITUAL HOUSE
SPIRITUAL SUBMISSION

STEPHEN KAUNG   SPIRITUAL KNOWLEDGE
SPIRITUAL POWER
SPIRITUAL REALITY
SPIRITUAL VALUE
SPIRITUAL BLESSING
SPIRITUAL DISCERNMENT

SPIRITUAL WARFARE
SPIRITUAL ASCENDANCY
SPIRITUAL MINDEDNESS
SPIRITUAL PERFECTION
SPIRITUAL FULNESS
SPIRITUAL SONSHIP
SPIRITUAL STEWARDSHIP
SPIRITUAL TRAVAIL
SPIRITUAL INHERITANCE
HARVEY CEDARS CONFERENCE:
HILE, KAUNG, LAMBERT
THE KING IS COMING

www.ingramcontent.com/pod-product-compliance
Lightning Source LLC
Chambersburg PA
CBHW060527030426
42337CB00015B/2008